Robert the Bruce

AND ALL THAT

Robert the Bruce

AND ALL THAT

Allan Burnett

Illustrated by Scoular Anderson

BIRLINN

First published in 2006 by
Birlinn Limited
West Newington House
10 Newington Road
Edinburgh
EH9 1QS

www.birlinn.co.uk

ISBN 10: 1 84158 497 5
ISBN 13: 978 1 84158 497 3

British Library Cataloguing-in-Publication Data
A catalogue record for this book is available from the British Library

Designed by James Hutcheson
Typeset by Iolaire Typesetting, Newtonmore
Printed and bound by Cox & Wyman Ltd, Reading

For my nephew
Alexander

Contents

The ground started trembling like jelly around King Robert the Bruce as he sat on his little grey pony. Thundering towards the king was an enemy knight on a giant heavy horse – aiming for the kill.

1

So did Bruce get out of the way? Not on your life.

The bloodthirsty knight gathered speed as he galloped closer, aiming his lance straight at Bruce's heart.

But did Bruce budge an inch? No chance.

As the lance's shining tip sped towards its target, it looked like Bruce would be skewered for sure.

What was Bruce waiting for? Well . . . he was waiting for the right moment to strike, of course.

Just as the knight was about to puncture him like a balloon, Bruce fooled his attacker by quickly sidestepping his pony out of harm's way.

Quick as a flash, Bruce stood up in his stirrups while the knight passed in front of him. Bruce then brought down his huge battleaxe upon his opponent's head.

Bruce's blade smashed through the knight's helmet and split his skull in two. The knight fell off his horse and into a lifeless, crumpled heap.

The knight had learned the hard way that you should

never, *ever* mess with King Robert the Bruce. But for those of you who would like to learn about Bruce the easy way, please read on.

As you have already gathered, Bruce was a quick-witted and mighty warrior. He was also Scotland's greatest king.

Born on 11 July 1274, Bruce would be more than 700 years old if he were still alive today. His armour would be very rusty.

Of course, Bruce is not around any more, but you can still find statues of him standing all over Scotland. By the way, not all Bruce statues are completely solid. When you look closer, some of them might be a bit wobbly.

Bruce's life story is a bit like his statues. Some bits of Bruce's story are true, which makes them solid. But some bits may or may not be true, which makes them wobbly.

Historians call the solid bits 'facts' and the wobbly bits 'legends'. Because Bruce's story is so old, and many facts about his life have gone missing or have been muddled up, there are lots of Bruce legends – and legends are not to be trusted.

These days, the legendary Bruce casts a long shadow over the real Bruce, like a stone statue towers over a real person.

But if it's the real Bruce you're after, don't panic. This book will help you to tell the difference between Bruce facts and Bruce legends while you follow his amazing real-life adventures.

By the way, going up real stone statues and wobbling them yourself is not recommended. You might end up like one of Bruce's enemies – splattered!

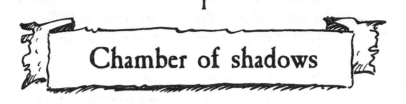

Chamber of shadows

To begin Bruce's story, let's turn our clocks back a few hundred years and imagine we are in the bedchamber where baby Bruce has just been born.

In the chamber are little baby Bruce and his mother, Marjorie, a tough Gaelic noblewoman – no doubt accompanied by midwives, maids and other courtiers.

Our picture of the chamber is very shadowy, but that's not because Marjorie gave birth by candlelight. It's because one of the most important bits of the picture is a legend.

You see, we don't know for sure which castle the chamber was in. In fact, we can't even be certain which country it was in!

Trouble is, there's no birth certificate stating plainly where Bruce was born. Instead, there are three legends:

1. Bruce might have been born at Lochmaben Castle in Annandale, which was a wild border country close to England. Bruce's dad's family had lived there for many years as Lords of Annandale.

2. On the other hand, Bruce might have tumbled out into the world next to skinned rabbits and plucked pheasants at a hunting lodge also owned by his dad. It was

in a place called Writtle, Essex, which is in southern England.

3. A third possibility is that Bruce was born at Turnberry Castle on Scotland's Ayrshire coast. This is the best bet.

Why is Turnberry the legend that's most likely to be true? Because it was in the earldom of Carrick, and Marjorie was the countess of Carrick.

In other words, Turnberry Castle was in Marjorie's ancestral homeland. It was the place where she probably felt safest and most secure. Oh, and it also had a very relaxing view of the pudding-shaped rock of Ailsa Craig, the beautiful island of Arran and the misty Mull of Kintyre.

In fair weather, you could even look across the sea to the kingdom of Ireland. A very pleasant spot for recuperating after you've just given birth to a king, wouldn't you say?

There's another important reason why Marjorie probably had her son on her own patch at Turnberry – she wore
the trousers in the Bruce household. If Marjorie wanted
her own way, she got it.

Unlike his wife and son, Bruce's dad was a weakling.
Apparently, he didn't even want to get married at all. The
rumour was that Marjorie locked him up until he agreed to
wed her!

All things considered, then, it is most likely that Bruce
was born in Turnberry – although we can't be certain.

Turnberry Castle is just a ruin now, next to a lighthouse.
If you ever go and visit it, though, you can imagine that it
was once a great fortress watched over by armed guards.
Turnberry was to play a very important role in Bruce's
grown-up adventures – but more about that later on.

If you want to get to know mediaeval (very old) heroes
like Bruce properly, the puzzle of Bruce's birthplace is the

kind of tricky problem you sometimes have to solve. Just make sure you think hard about the clues put before you and ask yourself which legend is most likely to be true?

Bruce admired people who could make up their own mind about things. If you were one of his knights, he would have relied on you to make tough decisions all the time.

But before Bruce could become king and get himself a squadron of knights, he had a lot of growing up to do.

2

Words of Wisdom

Lessons in duelling, horse riding, hunting and archery made growing up exciting for the young Bruce, and prepared him for life's adventures.

You'll have to be quicker than that, my young lord!

Bruce spent some of his youth in Scotland and some of it in England, since his parents owned estates in both countries. He was also sent on the odd trip to Ireland, a kingdom he would get to know well in later life.

He probably left home for a long time to live with another local family in the Gaelic neighbourhood of his mother, on Scotland's west coast and islands.

This living away from home was called fostering. It was common for Scottish clans or families to foster out their children to another clan.

Doing so showed you trusted another family to look after your own, and created a bond of friendship between two clans. It would have meant that lucky Bruce grew up with lots of brothers and sisters.

Young Bruce learned to speak many languages, too, which was a smart idea. This meant he could talk to people all over the kingdom of Scotland and people in foreign countries. More importantly, it meant people would really listen to what he had to say.

Each language Bruce learned gave him special powers, which would help him when he became king:

1. Bruce was taught Gaelic, which was his mother's native tongue. Gaelic was an ancient language used by people all over Scotland in those days. It was spoken in the neighbouring kingdom of Ireland, too.

Speaking Gaelic gave Bruce the power to unite people in Scotland and Ireland, doubling their strength. This was to be very important in later years, when Bruce was called upon to defend both kingdoms from attack – but more about that later.

2. Bruce was also taught Latin, which was a language used for all sorts of very important business, like worshipping God. Mediaeval Christians such as Bruce believed that God and some special members of His Church could perform real miracles – a bit like magic but more powerful.

Do you... dream of being a BIG SUCCESS?
Do you... want protection from your enemies?
Are you... keen to avoid the burning fires of HELL?
Then learn LATIN!

Et tu, Bruce!

Write Latin letters to the pope in Rome. The Pope is God's right-hand man, and leader of the Chistian Church. With the pope on your side, nobody can touch you!*

Write in Latin to your local branch of the Church. The leaders of your local Scottish branch are called bishops. Like the pope, bishops have special powers given to them by God. You'll be glad you've got a bishop behind you when the going gets tough!

Pray in Latin to the saints. The saints are the Heavenly ghosts of people from long ago, and were given supernatural powers by God for doing great or heroic things. Scotland has a few you can choose from, like Saint Columba, Saint Ninian and Saint Margaret. Send for the saints when you go into battle, and your enemies will wish they'd never been born!

* Warning: we cannot be held responsible if something you do or say upsets the pope, and he condemns you to roast in Hell for all eternity.

3. Bruce probably learned how to speak Inglis – which later became known as 'Scots'. Inglis was spoken by people in southern Scotland and northern England. It was useful to know Inglis if you wanted to raise an army or get supplies for Border wars.

That in thar tyme war wycht and wyse!

4. Finally, Bruce was taught Norman French, which was the language of his dad's early ancestors. Bruce learned that his first ancestor was a knight called Adam the Bruce, who built a castle at a place called Brus in Normandy.

In the Norman tongue, the Bruces called themselves 'de Brus', after the place where they originally came from. Because Adam came from Normandy, he was a Norman. Because Normandy is in France, he spoke Norman French. Simple, really.

Castel de Brus!

Like other Norman knights, the Bruces moved from Normandy to Scotland in search of land and good fortune. The Bruces were invited to settle in Annandale by Scotland's King David I – about 150 years before Robert the Bruce was born.

During those years, the Bruces of Annandale developed an annoying habit of always calling the eldest son of each generation Robert. Our hero was called Robert, but so was his dad. And his granddad. And his great-granddad. And his great-great granddad.

In fact our hero was no less than the EIGHTH Bruce of Annandale to be called Robert. Okay, so Robert is a nice name – but what's wrong with Kevin or Dave, or Engelbert?

Anyway, because all these Roberts passed on the Norman French tongue to our young hero, this would give him the power to influence important people who also had Norman French ancestors – such as the kings of England.

Mind you, sometimes languages alone were not enough to make sure other people listened to you. So Bruce needed weapons . . .

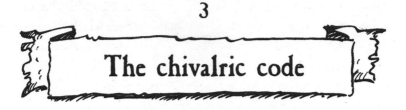

The chivalric code

We know what the young Bruce sounded like, then – but what did he look like? What handy moves did he learn with a sword?

After all, for Bruce, growing up was all about the thrill and romance of learning to be a knight. Knights got to carry fantastic weapons and wear great costumes.

Dressed in a coat of chain mail and armour plating, with roundels to protect his shoulders and elbows and a quilted tunic underneath to absorb the shock of sword blows, Bruce grew up to be a very impressive sight. He was mounted on a special, large horse called a destrier. A fully loaded destrier was very heavy – ideal for charging towards an enemy and splattering them!

Bruce also learned to ride nimble horses like ponies, and wear lighter armour made from boiled leather. He would discover that it was often better to be light and quick than heavy and slow.

Bruce wore a metal helmet called a bascinet, perhaps with a visor to cover his face. Underneath his helmet, we know he had strong cheekbones and even features.

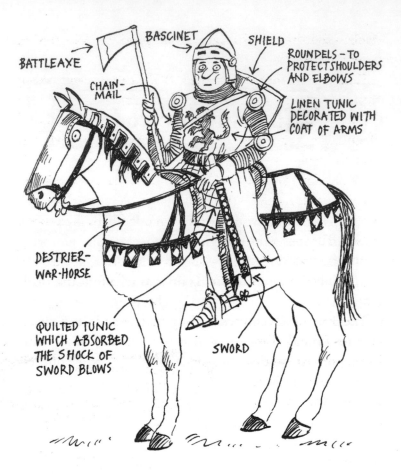

BATTLEAXE

BASCINET

SHIELD

CHAIN-MAIL

ROUNDELS – TO PROTECT SHOULDERS AND ELBOWS

LINEN TUNIC DECORATED WITH COAT OF ARMS

DESTRIER – WAR-HORSE

QUILTED TUNIC WHICH ABSORBED THE SHOCK OF SWORD BLOWS

SWORD

As a knight, Bruce would have taken part in jousting tournaments. In these tournaments he learned how to knock another knight off his horse with a lance, sword or other weapon.

Winning jousting competitions meant Bruce impressed other noble young men and fair young ladies. Young ladies were wooed by acts of bravery during tournaments and duels – and they liked knights to be good losers as well as good winners.

Knights like Bruce also had to learn to treat young women with courtesy, or good manners.

All of this was known as the chivalric code. It was a kind of guide to being a gentleman and was very popular in Bruce's day.

As a gallant young knight, Bruce took part in colourful pageants and processions. These pageants celebrated important events from the past with colourful banners, music, dancing and song.

In the evenings, Bruce was inspired and entertained from an early age by music – and tales about heroes from ages long past.

The ancient adventures of King Arthur and the Knights of the Round Table were popular stories. Bruce heard these around the banquet table at feasts, or in front of a crackling fire among friends.

A long, long time ago... in a Gaelic-sea far, far away...

Being a Scottish Gaelic knight, Bruce heard legendary Gaelic stories and songs, too. These awesome tales were about Scottish and Irish heroes like Oscar and

Fingal, who fought epic battles against evil villains.

Bruce heard tales, or sagas, about Viking warriors. These were fierce raiders who had once sailed across the North Sea to invade the coastal lands where Bruce was now growing up.

Living next to the sea taught Bruce how to handle himself on a ship just like a Viking, which was another important skill he would rely on later.

THE TYPE OF SHIP BRUCE SAILED WAS A BIRLINN. IT WAS EASIER TO TRAVEL BY SEA AS THERE WERE FEW ROADS. THE SEAS ON THE WEST COAST OF SCOTLAND WERE THE MOTORWAYS OF THEIR DAY.

I hate sailing in the rush hour!

With all the skills and knowledge he learned, Bruce was ready to look after the lands of Carrick and Annandale that his mum and dad would give him when they died.

There was also another thing that Bruce might inherit.

It had long been the dream of the Bruces that they would one day become kings of Scots. Bruce's royal blood came from King David I, the monarch who had first invited the Bruce family to Scotland all those years ago.

David I was Bruce's great-great-great-great-granddad (phew!), which sounds impressive. However, there were other people closer in line to the throne than Bruce and his family.

As a young boy, Bruce probably never thought he had a real chance of becoming king. When he was twelve, though, everything changed.

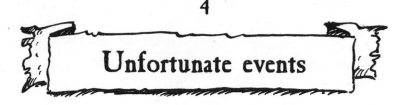

4

Unfortunate events

On the afternoon of 18 March 1286 a storm was brewing. Perhaps young Bruce was distracted from boring lessons as he looked out at the bad weather. Bruce could never have expected, though, that the tempest would leave Scotland in ruins.

The king of Scots at that time was Alexander III. He had ruled the nation happily for almost forty years and kept good neighbourly relations with England.

As long as Alexander didn't do anything stupid, all would remain well. So what would be an example of doing something stupid? Well, try racing your horse along the edge of a cliff. In a blizzard. In pitch dark.

That's exactly what Alexander did on that stormy night in 1286. And guess what? He got himself killed.

Exactly how it happened is a bit of a mystery. Alexander probably drank a fair bit of wine at a feast in Edinburgh Castle before he set out on his journey. Later, as he galloped along, the tipsy king was somehow thrown from his horse and died in the fall.

In fact, according to legend, Alexander rode straight off

a sea cliff and was splattered all over the beach below. Whichever way it happened, his dead body had to be scooped off the sand.

The Scots had hoped Alexander would leave behind a son who would be a good king. Unfortunately, all his children were dead. But he did have a very young granddaughter, Margaret, also known as the Maid of Norway.

Getting little Margaret over from Norway to Scotland in one piece would be very difficult. In those days, crossing the treacherous North Sea between the two countries was a matter or life or death. Even if her boat survived being shipwrecked, a wee lass like that was at great risk of becoming seriously ill during her long voyage.

Many Scots didn't expect the Maid of Norway to survive the journey. They were right. Before she reached mainland Scotland, Margaret became gravely sick and died. Her body was sailed back into the arms of her tearful dad, Erik II, the king of Norway.

Now the throne was empty, leaving the Scots with nobody in charge.

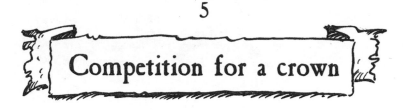

5

Competition for a crown

'So what do we do next?' the Scots began asking each other. An obvious solution would be to find a noble who was related to the royal family, and hand him the crown.

Why did the next king have to be a noble, though? Why not anybody who was smart and strong? Well, to understand this properly you need to imagine that Scotland was shaped like a giant pyramid (see the next page).

Eh? Look, it's simple, really. Imagine the king was the block at the top of the pyramid. Then you had the nobles, who were the blocks under him. And then, at the bottom, you had the common folk.

But what's this got to do with choosing a king? Well, if somebody wanted to have a chance of becoming king they needed to be near the top of the pyramid. In other words, they had to be a very important noble.

Even if somebody smart and strong at the bottom of the pyramid was related to the royals (highly unlikely), they had next to no chance of ever becoming king.

By the way, if you think the idea of a Scottish pyramid sounds daft, then think again. People in Bruce's day believed the Scots were related to the pharaohs of ancient Egypt – where pyramids were built.

KING HE WAS IN CHARGE OF THE COUNTRY. (QUEENS WERE NOT THOUGHT TO BE STRONG ENOUGH FOR THE JOB.)

NOBLES PEOPLE WHO OWNED OR CONTROLLED THE LAND WHICH THE COMMON FOLK LIVED ON.

THE MORE IMPORTANT THE NOBLE, THE BIGGER THE LAND.

WHEN THERE WAS TROUBLE THE NOBLES DECIDED WHO BECAME KING.

COMMON FOLK COOKS, FISHERMEN, CATTLE-HERDERS ETC. THEY HAD NO SAY IN WHO RAN SCOTLAND. THEY TOOK AN INTEREST IN WHAT WENT ON ABOVE THEM BECAUSE TROUBLE AT THE TOP MEANT EVEN BIGGER TROUBLE AT THE BOTTOM.

None of this really mattered when the crown could be handed down from one generation of the royal family to the next, which was nice and smooth.

But when things didn't run smoothly, like now, a new king had to be chosen from one of the noble families who were related to the royals. Like, say, the Bruces . . .

Great idea. But it had one small flaw – loads of nobles reckoned they had royal blood in their veins, not just the Bruces. All of them wanted a piece of the action.

There was somebody else, too, with his eyes on the Scottish throne. His name was Edward 'the Longshanks', ruler of the kingdom next door – England.

King Edward was nicknamed Longshanks because of his long legs ('shank' is an old word for the bit of your leg between your knee and your ankle). Longshanks had long fingers, too, and began wrapping these around the Scottish crown with schemes and plans.

In fact, Longshanks was a greedy king who dreamed of building an English empire across the whole British Isles.

Longshanks' empire would be like another pyramid built from the blocks of four smaller pyramids – England, Scotland, Wales and Ireland. Longshanks imagined himself sitting at the top, barking orders at everybody below and stamping on them if they didn't do as they were told.

The English king now had a chance to make his dream of conquering Scotland come true. Some of the Scots suggested that, because Longshanks was a neighbouring monarch, he should help pick their next king. Longshanks was happy to oblige and hatched a cunning plan:

> Dear Scots,
> Decide who should become King of Scots by holding a competition. The rules of the competition should be:
> 1 I make the rules
> 2 I judge the competition and pick the winner.
> 3 I change the rules when I feel like it.
> yours King Edward

The plan went like clockwork. The Scots agreed to hold a competition for the crown and let Longshanks pick the winner. Two competitors quickly entered the contest:

Then came the really cunning part of the plan. Longshanks encouraged lots of other nobles to enter the competition, even though their claims to the throne were rubbish compared to Bruce's granddad and Balliol. So what was so cunning about this? Well, if there were three or more competitors, the law said that they would all have to swear allegiance to the judge – yes, that's Longshanks. This meant the winning competitor would have to do anything Longshanks said!

The competitors thought about this for a while and said, 'No chance.'

So Longshanks moved a large and threatening English army up to the border with Scotland. The competitors thought about this for a while and then said, 'Er, all right then.'

Eventually, in November 1292, news came that Longshanks had picked Balliol as the winner.

Bruce's granddad was outraged, and vowed that the Bruces must never give up trying to win the Scottish crown. But he felt he was past it, so he turned to Bruce's dad and said something like:

I'm getting too old for this! You take over the claim for the crown, son.

Meanwhile, Balliol had problems of his own – Longshanks had started bullying him.

Dear Balliol,
Here is my two-point plan for keeping the Scots under control:

[1] You might be King of Scots but you do what I say, okay?

[2] Send all Scotland's treasures to me.

yours, King Edward

Balliol grumbled but he went along with Longshanks' demands – until he was commanded to join Longshanks in a war against France.

The Scots and Balliol got on with France very well, thanks very much. So instead of helping Longshanks, they said to the French:

This was the beginning of a beautiful friendship between Scotland and France which became known as the Auld Alliance. But it was also the beginning of something rather more unpleasant . . .

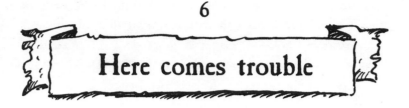

6

Here comes trouble

So how did Longshanks feel when the Scots refused to do as they were told, then? You guessed it – he was steaming with rage. He decided to stop mucking about and just invade Scotland.

Longshanks rolled his English army across southern Scotland like a giant lawnmower. The Scots were sliced, chopped and hacked up just like thousands of tiny blades of grass. This was the beginning of Scotland's War of Independence.

The Scots were ready to fight Longshanks, but King Balliol wasn't. He chickened out and surrendered to Longshanks at Montrose.

Longshanks tore off Balliol's royal jacket, forced him to resign as King of Scots and then booted him into a prison. (For a while, at any rate. He was released later.)

IMPORTANT NOTICE

SCOTLAND NOW UNDER ENGLISH OCCUPATION

yours Longshanks

So what Scotland needed now was a hero to step forward and fight for freedom. Enter William Wallace, a hero who was so great that you can read all about him in his very own book – *William Wallace And All That*!

Wallace won lots of battle against the English – but was he helped or hindered by Robert the Bruce?

Bruce couldn't make up his mind what to do.

For several years Bruce went back and forth – one moment on Wallace's side, the next on Longshanks' side.

Then, in 1305, something happened that forced Bruce to decide which side he was really on: Wallace was executed by Longshanks. Bits of Wallace's body were stuck on spikes at Berwick, Perth and Stirling.

Wallace's gruesome execution was a warning from Longshanks to anybody else who had ideas about being a rebel. So who is the last person you might expect to have ignored that warning and put his life on the line by leading a new rebellion? Here are a couple of clues:

Clue #1   Unlike Wallace, he had been very careful until now to make sure he didn't upset Longshanks too much.

Clue #2   His dad had just died in 1304, leaving him a claim to the throne of Scotland.

It's Robert the Bruce – our hero!

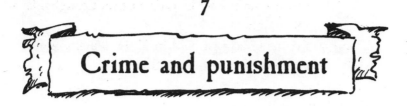

7

Crime and punishment

Thanks to poor old Wallace's execution, Bruce realised that Longshanks had absolutely no intention of ever allowing the Scots to have a proper king of their own. In fact, it was now obvious to Bruce that Longshanks wanted every last Scot to be hanged, crushed, split, stabbed or splattered so he could steal their land.

Bruce saw which path he had to go down. To become king, he had to get rid of the English once and for all!

Great, except there were two large problems Bruce had to solve first. Here's what he might have been thinking to himself:

By the winter of 1305, the first problem looked to be taking care of itself. Longshanks was in his mid-sixties, which was very old indeed by mediaeval standards, and definitely on his last legs.

The second problem was trickier, though, because John Comyn of Badenoch had a famously fiery temper. In fact, Bruce and Comyn had already come to blows once before.

Comyn had accused Bruce of plotting against Balliol and grabbed him by the throat. The two men had started brawling and had had to be separated.

But that was a few years ago. Maybe Comyn had mellowed out since then?

This must have been what Bruce was thinking when he sent out a secret invitation to Comyn, which went something like this:

Dear John Comyn,
We need to talk. Meet me at
Greyfriars Church in Dumfries
on 10 February 1306.
(Throw this letter in the fire – no one
else should know about this!)
        Yours, secretly
Robert the Bruce

Greyfriars Church was a very risky place to plot a rebellion. It was right under the ramparts of Dumfries Castle, which was home to a garrison of English soldiers.

But if Bruce persuaded Comyn to join him, they could celebrate by striking out together to capture the castle. It would make a glorious start to the rebellion and people across Scotland would rally to the cause.

Except things didn't quite go according to plan. Comyn turned up as agreed on that cold winter day, but it seems he soon started to warm up the chapel with his hot temper.

Exactly what happened when the two men came face to face is not clear. It seems that while they were at the high altar of the church, right under God's nose, Bruce offered

Comyn lands in return for supporting Bruce's quest to become king.

The angry Comyn would have none of this and threw Bruce's offer back in his face. This was a great insult to Bruce. Soon, fists were flying.

This time, though, Comyn would not get the chance to try strangling Bruce as he had done in the past. In the scuffle that followed, in front of the holy altar, Bruce stabbed Comyn with a dagger.

Comyn ended up dead. But the question is, did Bruce mean to kill Comyn? Or was Bruce just trying to defend himself?

If we imagine Bruce was tried in court for murder, the case for the prosecution might have gone something like this:

So what would be the case for the defence? Well, Bruce's lawyer might have argued something like this:

Murder means planning to deliberately kill someone – but can we be sure that is what Bruce was up to? The incident is a mystery to this day. The church where it happened is long gone, although it is still a holy site. Until somebody digs up conclusive evidence, the judgement is up to you.

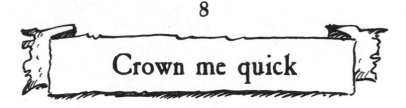

8

Crown me quick

With Comyn dead, a big obstacle was now removed from Bruce's path. Bruce and his followers immediately seized Dumfries Castle from the English and struck out to take control of south-west Scotland.

Unfortunately, another obstacle had unexpectedly survived the winter and was still in the land of the living – Longshanks. Bruce knew Longshanks would be spitting blood after he heard about what had happened, so Bruce had no time to lose.

Bruce had to recruit a Scottish army to follow him into battle against Longshanks – and he had to do it quickly.

What was the best way of doing this? Bruce would get himself crowned King of Scots, of course.

This was not as easy as it sounds. Without another king, like Longshanks, to give Bruce his blessing, Bruce would have to try to find other powerful people to make him King of Scots.

So Bruce called on the help of two wise men. These were Bishop Lamberton of St Andrews and Bishop Wishart of Glasgow, the two most powerful churchmen in Scotland – with special powers given to them by God.

Lamberton and Wishart didn't like Longshanks and they didn't like him trampling over Scotland, or the Scottish Church. They saw that Bruce was smart and strong, and wanted to help him become king and drive out the English.

Wishart got to work by 'absolving' Bruce of the sin of killing Comyn in a church. So what does 'absolving' mean? It means that Wishart used his special powers to forgive Bruce on God's behalf.

This forgiveness was essential if Bruce was to become king and recruit an army. Nobody would want to fight for someone who had upset God by killing another man in a holy place, even if it was in self defence. In a way, absolution was a bit like a spell that restored Bruce's reputation as a good person and protected his soul from going to Hell after he died.

Bruce was then crowned King Robert I at Scone Abbey near Perth, on New Year's Day, 1306.

Hang on a minute – how could it be New Year's Day if Comyn had been killed in February? Well, a lot has changed in seven hundred years. In Bruce's day even the calendar was different.

Today we use what's called the Gregorian calendar, with the new year starting on 1 January. In Bruce's day, though, Scotland used an old method of calculating dates called the Julian calendar.

In the Julian calendar, New Year's Day was on 25 March – which was when Christians believed the Virgin Mary learned she would give birth to the son of God. Now it was also to become the day when Bruce would be reborn as King Robert I, a king whose mission was to restore peace and happiness to Scotland.

A small band of friends and supporters gathered around Bruce in Scone Abbey, along with his wife, Elizabeth, and his brothers and sisters.

Wishart dressed Bruce in Scotland's royal robes, which had been kept safe from Longshanks in a chest. Then, according to legend, the countess of Buchan, a brave woman, put a crown of gold upon Bruce's head.

After a blessing from the bishops, the 31-year-old Bruce could finally call himself Robert I, King of Scots.

So did Bruce then rule happily ever after? Of course not. His struggle for Scotland was only just beginning . . .

9

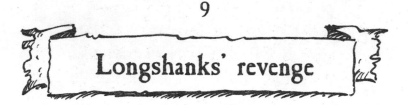

Longshanks' revenge

Bruce might have been a king to some Scots, but to others he was now a dangerous villain.

They believed he had killed Comyn in cold blood and stolen Balliol's throne.

Bruce now had a long, hard road ahead of him – with big obstacles blocking his way.

The first obstacles were the friends of Comyn and Balliol. They wanted revenge and would not rest until Bruce was dead, simple as that.

Then there was old Longshanks, who was still refusing to croak. When the king of England heard what Bruce had been up to, he was so enraged he almost jumped out of his wrinkly skin.

Longshanks wasted little time in dashing off letters to the pope, explaining that Bruce had killed Comyn in a church. He demanded that the pope hand Bruce a severe punishment.

Longshanks' letters were full of nasty things about Bruce and went something like this:

Dear Pope Clement V

Robert the Bruce has committed a terrible <u>crime</u> against GOD and His Church. We humbly request that your Holiness has BRUCE <u>excommunicated</u>.

You know, <u>ex-comm-uni-cated</u> —which means the rascal won't have the help and protection of the Church EVER AGAIN!! It also means his <u>soul</u> will be condemned to the burning fires of <u>HELL</u>

We will do everything in our power to make sure Bruce ends up in Hell as <u>quickly</u> <u>as</u> <u>possible</u>

Bruce now calls himself <u>Robert King of Scots</u> ~ but he has no right to do that <u>without</u> <u>my</u> <u>permission</u>!!!

So we have charged him with treason against the English Crown which is punishable by DEATH. We have issued a warrant for Bruce's arrest and we will deal with him the same way we dealt with that other Scottish upstart-William Wallace.

Thanks for your attention in this matter.

Yours sincerely

King Edward Longshanks

P.S. Happy New Year!

Longshanks knew the pope needed English men and money for fighting holy wars against enemies in distant lands. So Longshanks wasn't surprised when the pope duly obliged and Bruce was excommunicated.

Excommunication was a bit like a powerful curse from the pope. It totally destroyed Wishart's absolution that had been protecting Bruce. When Bruce found out about the curse, he knew he would have to race against time to break it before he died and was condemned to Hell. And with the king of England and at least half of Scotland after his blood, Bruce knew he might end up in Hell sooner rather than later.

Right on cue, Longshanks decreed that his son Prince Edward should be knighted and sent north to Scotland. Prince Edward would lead an army of three hundred eager young knights with orders to track Bruce down.

But Longshanks didn't have much confidence in his son . . .

So Sir Aymer de Valence, the Earl of Pembroke, galloped north with 3,000 horsemen to see if he could capture Bruce first. When he got to Scotland, Valence was joined by many of the dead Comyn's friends, all bursting to give Bruce a battering.

Prince Edward and Valence also had an instruction from Longshanks for what to do when they came across any of Bruce's friends. What do you think that instruction was? Was it:

Yes, the answer was of course C – to be done as painfully as possible, please.

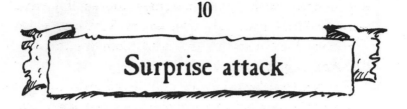

10

Surprise attack

While the English army was rumbling northward, Bruce galloped around northern Scotland looking for anyone who would fight for him. Eventually, Bruce gathered together an army of 4,500 soldiers. Good for Bruce.

However, Valence turned up at the city of Perth with an army that had now snowballed to 6,000 men. Not good for Bruce.

The townspeople of Perth gulped in terror and let Valence roll through the city gates without putting up a fight.

But Valence had no time to make himself comfortable before Bruce turned up outside the city walls, determined to snatch Perth back out of English control.

To capture the town, Bruce had to follow the rules of the chivalric code he had learned as a young knight. If Bruce had kept a copy of the code in his pocket, it might have read something like this:

```
PAGE 27
RULES FOR CAPTURING A TOWN FROM OPPONENT.

THERE IS A TWO-STEP PROCEDURE:

1  CHALLENGE OPPONENT TO SURRENDER
   TOWN PEACEFULLY.

2  IF HE REFUSES, CHALLENGE HIM TO COME
   OUTSIDE TOWN WALLS AND FIGHT.  WINNER
   GETS TOWN.
```

Bruce sent a message to Valence giving him the two options. Valence replied by saying that he would come out and fight tomorrow morning.

Satisfied that Valence's intentions were honourable, Bruce turned his army around and trotted off to camp for the night a few miles away in a place called Methven.

Just as Bruce and his men were getting ready for bed, they were suddenly taken by surprise. Valence had tricked Bruce, and followed him.

Valence and his troop of assassins pounced on Bruce's sleepy soldiers. Without their swords or horses at the ready, Bruce's men were easy meat for the attackers. The victims were skewered, strangled or scrunched under hooves. Many others were captured.

Somehow, Bruce and a small band of Scottish knights managed to escape into the night. Yet it was a dreadful defeat for the new King of Scots.

News of Valence's victory soon reached Prince Edward, whose army was further south. Now that Valence had

done the dirty work, Prince Edward and his knights celebrated by riding around southern Scotland and slaughter-
ing just about every living thing in their path.

11

On the run

Bruce was now in deep trouble. He was wanted by Long-shanks for murder and treason, and he was cursed by the pope. His army had just been cut to pieces, and all he had left was a small band of followers.

The King of Scots knew he had to escape to a place where he would be safe from Longshanks' clutches. So he decided to ride west, over the hills and far away to the coastal hideouts he had known as a boy. Bruce was sure he would find some people there to help him.

The hard part was getting there. Death lurked around every corner, in the shape of loyal friends of Balliol or Comyn. The country was also swarming with English soldiers.

It was not long before Bruce and his band rode into trouble. As they headed through a narrow gap called the Pass of Dalry, some friends of Comyn ambushed them.

According to legend, the attackers came down on the king's party like an avalanche, running at the horses and riders with their axes. Many of Bruce's band were slain, but others managed to scramble to safety.

IT'S SAID THAT BRUCE BLOCKED THE ATTACKERS HIMSELF, ALLOWING THE OTHERS TO ESCAPE. WITH SEVERAL MIGHTY STROKES OF HIS SWORD, HE CUT DOWN MORE THAN A DOZEN OF HIS ENEMIES. THIS STORY MIGHT BE DODGY AS WE'RE NOT SURE IF IT'S TRUE.

Bruce now realised his loved ones were in grave danger. So he instructed his younger brother Neil and the loyal earl of Atholl to escort his wife, Elizabeth, daughter Marjorie and other loyal women like the countess of Buchan away to a place of safety.

But they didn't get far before they were all captured by the English army. A blacksmith had helped the English find them in return for a reward of gold.

The English gave the blacksmith his reward all right – but as a drink?! The story goes that the gold was heated until it became molten liquid. Then it was poured down the screaming blacksmith's throat – because nobody likes a traitor.

Neil and Atholl were executed and their heads stuck up on poles. All of Bruce's women were put in prison – with Bruce's poor sister Mary and the countess of Buchan locked in cages hanging from the walls of Roxburgh and Berwick castles.

Bruce himself would not discover what had happened until later. In the meantime, he and his men decided to avoid capture by going underground – which means moving about quietly without being noticed.

Bruce and his men dumped their armour, waved good-bye to their horses and moved about from place to place on foot dressed like everyday, common folk. It was a good way of not drawing attention to themselves, but it was also a bit like being on a holiday where they had to stay at the worst hotels in the world:

Bruce and his men went for miles from place to place, zigzagging around the south-western fringe of the kingdom. Eventually they reached Dunaverty Castle on the Mull of Kintyre, which was right at the fingertip of mainland Scotland.

There Bruce hid until he could escape to somewhere even Longshanks' long arms couldn't reach him.

When Valence learned Bruce was at Dunaverty Castle, he gave chase. By the time the English commander arrived there, however, Bruce had vanished.

For the next five months, Bruce was nowhere to be found. So where was he? And what was he up to?

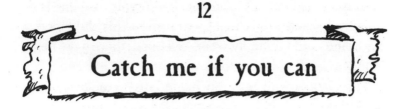

12

Catch me if you can

Bruce probably escaped from his pursuers by setting sail for a mysterious boot-shaped island between Scotland and Ireland called Rathlin. There he found a good place to hide, some decent food and time to heal his wounds.

During the winter and spring of 1307, it seems Bruce stayed on Rathlin but also visited many Scottish islands.

When Longshanks heard Bruce was in the isles, he ordered ships to hunt down the renegade king – but Bruce hopped from island to island, so they couldn't find him.

All the while he was probably thinking about how to win over his kingdom, and looking for people to help him. Luckily, because Bruce had spent some of his childhood in the islands and his family were well liked, there were many islanders he could turn to now in his hour of need.

The islander who probably helped Bruce the most was a powerful woman called Christina MacRuari, also known as the Lady of Garmoran.

Christina encouraged her king to fight back by helping him raise an army of island warriors with great warships called birlinns.

Soon Bruce must have felt felt refreshed and ready to take on Longshanks' army once more. He sent his brothers Thomas and Alexander on a mission to the Scottish mainland against the English.

The brothers boldly set out with hundreds of men in eighteen birlinns – but sailed into a trap. While trying to get ashore, they were ambushed by friends of the dead Comyn.

Thomas and Alexander were taken south to Carlisle where Longshanks was hungrily awaiting them. They were both butchered.

News soon reached Bruce of the catastrophe. Before long he also learned that his other brother, Neil, had been killed – and his beloved women all imprisoned.

Bruce must have been devastated by all this. According to legend, he crawled off to lie down in an island cave . . . and wept.

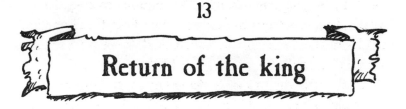

13

Return of the king

The king lay alone in the darkness of his cave for a while, thinking about whether to give up his quest and leave Scotland forever. Then something extraordinary happened – a spider crept up and turned him into . . . a guerrilla.

DO NOT CONFUSE **GUERRILLAS** WITH **GORILLAS**

GORILLA – BIG HAIRY APE

GUERRILLA – A SOLDIER WHO MAKES SURPRISE ATTACKS ON THE ENEMY – (THE WORD IS SPANISH AND MEANS 'LITTLE ARMY')

A guerrilla is a fighter who attacks a much bigger and more powerful enemy by making lots of small, surprise attacks. In other words, he uses his mind instead of his muscles to win battles – whereas gorillas probably do things the other way around.

So where does the spider come in? According to legend, while Bruce rested on his back he spotted a tiny spider out of the corner of his eye.

The creature was struggling to make its web by swinging a thread from the ceiling to the cave wall. It tried and tried again, at least seven or eight times, until eventually it succeeded.

Bruce thought about this for a while. That tiny spider had been determined never to give up, no matter how hard things got. Surely a king shouldn't give up when the going gets tough, either? 'If an insect can be that strong,' Bruce thought, 'so can I.'

So the spider made Bruce decide to battle on. Or did it? Well, the legend of the spider is probably not true. In fact, some people say it's just a web of fantasy that was made up later on.

On the other hand, there are lots of spiders on Rathlin Island. So it would be equally silly to insist that Bruce definitely never saw one while he was there. Who knows?

He may not have seen a spider in his cave, but Bruce definitely hatched a secret guerrilla plan to win back Scotland. Instead of trying to win large battles, which is what knights like him were used to, Bruce decided to concentrate on small, swift, secretive strikes – preferably while his enemies were asleep, relaxing or EVEN ON THE TOILET! In other words, Bruce realised he had to ditch the chivalric code for a while and stop being Mr Nice Guy.

We also know for sure that Bruce was encouraged not to give up, and instead fight back as a guerrilla in the spring of 1307, by at least two important people. One of them was Christina, the Lady of Garmoran. There may even have been a tingle of romance between Christina and the King.

The other person who encouraged Bruce was a young, foolhardy and incredibly courageous Scottish noble called Sir James Douglas. Douglas came from a rich and powerful family who owned lots of land near the border with England.

As part of Bruce's outlaw band, Douglas was like a cowboy in Scotland's Wild West. He rustled (stole) cattle, robbed castles, slashed or shot his enemies with swords and arrows – and generally behaved like a bandit.

With loyal and courageous friends like Douglas and Christina, Bruce could press ahead with new plans to invade the mainland.

First, he had to win back his homeland of Carrick from English control. So he bid farewell to Christina and his other island friends and set sail for Turnberry Castle.

When they arrived, it is said that Bruce and his men found the whole of Carrick swarming with English soldiers. So Bruce waited until nightfall and then sneaked into Turnberry village, where the English soldiers guarding the castle lay sleeping.

Remembering what Longshanks' forces had done to his own loved ones, Bruce and his men turned the enemy soldiers into mincemeat. The return of the king had begun.

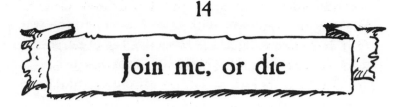

14

Join me, or die

News that Bruce was back in business soon reached the fearsome commander Valence. He vowed to sort Bruce out, but instead Valence's men got thumped twice:

BATTLE **1** GLEN TROOL. BRUCE BEAT 1,500 ENGLISH KNIGHTS BY FIRING AN ARROW THROUGH THEIR LEADER'S THROAT AND MAKING THE REST OF THEM GALLOP OFF IN PANIC.

BATTLE **2** LOUDEN HILL. BRUCE AND HIS MEN DUG LOTS OF HOLES IN THE GROUND BEFORE THE BATTLE THEN COVERED THEM WITH BRUSHWOOD. WHEN THE ENGLISH CAVALRY FELL INTO THESE TRAPS, THE SCOTS SKEWERED THEM WITH SPEARS.

It was two–nil to Bruce and Valence was mortified – but not half as much as his master, Longshanks. Still clinging onto life by his fingernails, the decrepit king of England decided that if he wanted a job done well, he would have to do it himself.

Longshanks rode north with a fresh force, but he was gravely ill. He got as far as the border village of Burgh-on-Sands before he died, on 7 July 1307. That was just a few days before Bruce's birthday – but it's unlikely the news spoiled his party.

Yet not even death could stop Longshanks trying to batter Bruce. Before he died, Longshanks ordered that his body be boiled in a giant cauldron. Once the flesh had melted away, Longshanks' bones were to be plucked out and put in a casket – then taken into battle against the Scots.

Happily for Bruce, Longshanks' remains never saw any real action. The old tyrant's body was abandoned by his son and heir, Prince Edward (who now became Edward II). Edward II wanted to get back to the safety of southern England as soon as possible.

The fact that Longshanks' son was now on the English throne was great news for Bruce because Edward II:

1 PREFERRED PRANCING AROUND THE PALACE WITH HIS PALS.

2 PREFERRED BRICKLAYING TO BATTLES.

3 ANNOYED SO MANY PEOPLE IN ENGLAND THAT HE HAD PLENTY OF ENEMIES AT HOME TO BOTHER ABOUT.

That meant Bruce was free to turn most of his attention towards some unfinished business in the north of Scotland.

This part of the country was home to many Scots who were friends and relatives of the dead Comyn and the banished Balliol. They all hated Bruce, and wished Edward II's army would come back and crush him.

With no time to lose, Bruce marched north to sort out the Comyn and Balliol supporters. On the way, he smashed Urquhart Castle into ruins on the shore of Loch Ness. Even the Loch Ness monster would have swum away in terror!

Destroying castles instead of capturing them was another guerrilla trick. It meant your enemy couldn't come back and use them. And Bruce didn't need castles anyway, now that Scottish people were flocking to join him from all the corners of the kingdom.

When Bruce got to the homeland of the Comyns he burned everything in his path. Then Bruce pounced on Aberdeen, which gave him control over a very important sea port.

To encourage old enemies to become friends, Bruce held a big meeting of nobles and churchmen from all over the kingdom. The meeting was called a parliament, and was important for three reasons:

1. It showed Bruce was a king who listened to the views of people below him in the Scottish pyramid. Not quite democracy, but getting there.
2. It showed other countries that the Scots just wanted to be left in peace to run their own country. The kings of France and Norway began to take notice of this, and recognised Bruce as king of Scots.
3. All in all it showed that Bruce meant business, which encouraged the Scottish people to really get behind him.

The parliament got in touch with Edward II:

So it was back out on the road again for Bruce, as he continued clearing out the English garrisons and their remaining Scottish supporters.

In 1313, Bruce led his men as they waded across the moat under the walls of Perth – a town that was still held by the English.

Bruce was reportedly the first to climb up the ladder scaling the walls and jump down into the town, his sword at the ready. As his men poured down behind him, Bruce hacked and slashed at the enemy soldiers inside. Soon the English were driven out.

That same year, news reached Bruce that Balliol had finally died of old age on his estates in France. Bruce was now only one short step away from being the undisputed king of Scots.

Soon the only major English stronghold left north of the border was the mighty Stirling Castle. The English soldiers inside were completely cut off and isolated from the nearest friendly castle, which was Berwick – several days' march away, on the border.

Although Stirling was a great fortress, it was besieged by the Scots. Gripped by fear, the English castle constable, Sir Philip de Mowbray, might have looked up his own copy of the chivalric code for some advice on what to do next:

PAGE 46
WHAT TO DO WHEN YOUR CASTLE IS UNDER SIEGE:

MAKE AN AGREEMENT WITH THE BESIEGERS THAT YOU WILL HAND OVER THE CASTLE ON A CERTAIN DATE – UNLESS AN ARMY OF REINFORCEMENTS COME TO YOUR AID.

IF THE REINFORCEMENTS ARRIVE ON TIME, THE BESIEGERS WILL HAVE TO FIGHT FOR THE CASTLE.

IMPORTANT NOTE: DON'T FORGET TO SEND A MESSENGER FOR HELP BEFORE YOU MAKE ANY AGREEMENT WITH THE ENEMY!!

De Mowbray followed these instructions to the letter, and first sent for help from Edward II.

Bruce now remembered his own chivalrous training and honourably agreed to a deadline of Midsummer's Day – 24 June 1314. He felt his own army might now be ready to face the English in a traditional large battle.

When Edward II received de Mowbray's message, he was urged by his nobles and generals to get tough with Bruce. 'Send north the largest army England can muster,' they cried, 'crush the Scots once and for all.'

The stage was now set for a showdown – the greatest battle in Scottish history!

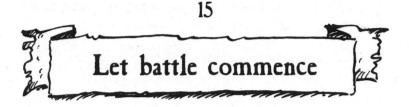

15

Let battle commence

On Midsummer's Eve, the day before the deadline, the soldiers in Stirling Castle were marooned. This didn't mean they were painted a funny colour, it meant they were completely alone and cut off from their friends. They were an English island in a sea of angry Scots.

The worried soldiers looked out from the castle ramparts and saw two armies gathered below on the boggy field of Bannockburn, just a few miles to the south. The armies' colourful flags were clearly visible, fluttering in the breeze.

SITE of the BATTLE of BANNOCKBURN

RIVER FORTH

STIRLING CASTLE

SCOTTISH CAMP

SCOTTISH ARMY

BOG

THE BANNOCK BURN

BOG

BOG

BOG

ENGLISH ARMY

Historians often argue about exactly where the two armies were, as well as what happened next, but it probably went something like this. On one side was Edward II, who had arrived with reinforcements just in the nick of time. On the other side was Bruce, who would now have to fight for the castle as agreed.

Bruce's chances of success didn't look good. Edward II may not have been the great war leader his dad Longshanks had been, but Edward II's army was much, much larger than Bruce's. It was like a gang of giants, compared to a handful of dwarves.

Just about every able fighting man in the whole of England and Wales had been commanded to turn up for this battle. The English army numbered a whopping 15,000 men at least.

On top of that, Edward II was blessed with some excellent generals – provided he listened to their advice.

He also had some awesome weapons. Take a look:

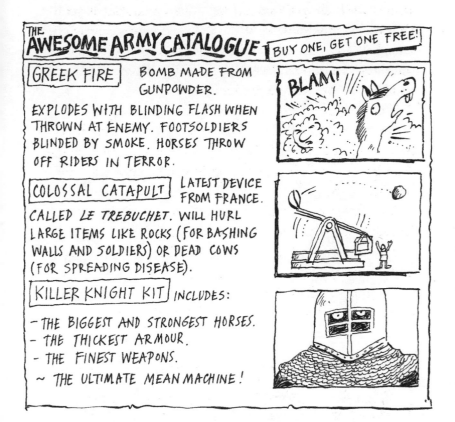

THE AWESOME ARMY CATALOGUE — BUY ONE, GET ONE FREE!

GREEK FIRE — BOMB MADE FROM GUNPOWDER.
EXPLODES WITH BLINDING FLASH WHEN THROWN AT ENEMY. FOOTSOLDIERS BLINDED BY SMOKE. HORSES THROW OFF RIDERS IN TERROR.

BLAM!

COLOSSAL CATAPULT — LATEST DEVICE FROM FRANCE. CALLED *LE TREBUCHET*. WILL HURL LARGE ITEMS LIKE ROCKS (FOR BASHING WALLS AND SOLDIERS) OR DEAD COWS (FOR SPREADING DISEASE).

KILLER KNIGHT KIT INCLUDES:
- THE BIGGEST AND STRONGEST HORSES.
- THE THICKEST ARMOUR.
- THE FINEST WEAPONS.
~ THE ULTIMATE MEAN MACHINE!

Bruce, on the other hand, had only light cavalry and fewer than 6,000 foot-soldiers. Instead of the heavy armour made from chain mail and metal plates worn by the English, Bruce's best men wore cheaper armour made from hard-boiled leather.

Leather armour made the Scots look cool and mean, but it was still easier to pierce with a sword than metal.

Luckily, the king of Scots had some cunning tricks up his sleeve to help his men. These tricks all began with the letter 'M', and were as follows:

1. **Miracles** - Bruce brought some bones of great Scottish saints to the battlefield in little metal boxes. Bruce's loyal bishops said prayers in Latin over the bones, so that the saints would help the Scots during the battle.

One of these saints was called Columba, who was known to have been very handy with a sword when he was alive. Bruce and his men believed that Columba's spirit would fight for them now in their hour of need.

2. **Marshes** - Bruce blocked Edward II's path by positioning his own army in an area full of deep, boggy marshes. To get past the Scots and reach the castle, Edward II's men and horses would have to struggle over the squelchy, treacherous bog - leaving them exhausted.

Bruce and his men also laid other traps for the English to fall into, like digging holes and covering them with brushwood. More importantly, Bruce didn't forget to leave his own soldiers an escape route to the north – just in case they had to retreat.

3. Morale – Bruce and his men had very good morale. This meant that they had a strong fighting spirit and a belief that they deserved to win. If ever you have good morale you are half way to winning a battle already.

In fact, Bruce gave his men a fantastic morale boost when the two armies warmed up with a small battle on Midsummer's Eve before the main battle on Midsummer's Day. During the fighting on Midsummer's Eve, Bruce amazed everyone with his mastery of hand-to-hand combat.

The excitement happened when one of the English knights spotted Bruce in an isolated spot, away from his men and mounted on only a small grey pony.

The knight was called Sir Henry de Bohun. He was the commander of the English vanguard, meaning he was in charge of the men at the front of the English army. When he saw that Bruce was a sitting duck, de Bohun realised that killing the king of Scots now would make him a hero back in England.

So de Bohun seized his chance and went at Bruce as if in a jousting competition – only this time it was a fight to the death. As he thundered towards Bruce, de Bohun lowered his lance for the kill.

But de Bohun was the knight that you read about at the beginning of Bruce's story, so guess what happened next . . .

Just in time, Bruce saw what was coming. He and his little pony neatly sidestepped the charging English knight and Bruce sprang up in his stirrups to strike back.

In one mighty stroke, Bruce's battleaxe came down on de Bohun's helmet and sliced into his head like it was a pumpkin. It was first blood to Bruce – and his men must have cheered with joy (and relief).

That day came to an end with many poor English horses killed, as their riders tangled unsuccessfully with the Scots' giant hedgehogs.

Hedgehogs? Well, they weren't real hedgehogs. They were soldiers carrying very long spears, or pikes, who bunched together with their spears sticking out. So when they moved around as one, they looked like a giant . . . hedgehog. (Just a lot more frightening than the ones at the bottom of your garden.)

The other word for these 'hedgehogs' was schiltroms (or schiltrons). If a knight dared to charge into a schiltrom, the

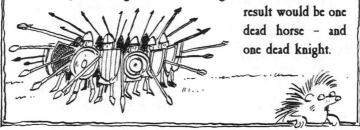

result would be one dead horse – and one dead knight.

So the Scots showed they were no pushovers, but Edward II wasn't impressed. He was confident that his men would crush the Scots in a full battle the next day – and make giant hedgehogs extinct.

As night fell, Edward II's wise generals advised that he should not try to move any of his army across the treacherous, marshy bog to get nearer the Scots. It would make the English soldiers tired and easier to attack in the morning.

Remember, though, Edward II was a complete twit. So he did exactly the opposite of what his sensible advisers suggested.

Edward II ordered a large portion of his army to cross the deadly marshes in the darkness. Edward II himself stayed safely where he was, of course – surrounded by bodyguards in a marquee back on nice dry ground.

Meanwhile, his grumbling men had to go to local houses and steal doors and bits of roof, so they could be brought back and used to make primitive bridges over the bog.

At least the locals, now in very draughty and wet houses, could comfort themselves with the knowledge that they would still get a better night's sleep than the soldiers.

Back on the marshes, the English soldiers and horses slipped, slithered and scrambled their way across. Eventually they got to the other side – but they were now cold, wet and miserable.

Terrified of sleeping so close to the enemy, the English soldiers lay down to rest with their swords and horses kept at the ready. It's unlikely anybody had their eyes shut for long.

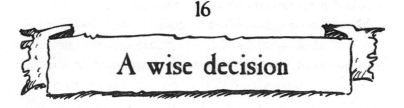

16

A wise decision

The cold, wet and terrified English soldiers might have been in higher spirits if they had known that Bruce was also having a sleepless night.

In fact, the king of Scots was thinking about retreating. Although he had scored a success the day before, the sheer size of the English army made Bruce think that a full battle might be too risky.

Then something made him change his mind. A Scottish knight who had been supporting the English came over to Bruce's side and brought good news. The knight explained that the English were absolutely miserable and had very poor morale.

This news made Bruce realise that the English had fallen into his trap – the marshes had bogged them down and worn them out. He now knew that the Scots stood a good chance of victory, so he decided to stay put and wait for sunrise.

When dawn broke on Midsummer's Day, the time for warming up and preparing was over. It was now time for the real battle to commence. Bruce and his men knelt to pray to God – because they knew many of them would be knocking on the gates of Heaven before the day was out.

According to reports, Edward II saw the Scots doing this and thought they were actually kneeling before *him*.

This showed that Edward II really was a very vain and arrogant king, in his fancy silk underwear and polished armour plates. He turned to one of his commanders, Sir Ingram de Umfraville:

'So be it,' said the king of England – and ordered his men to attack. The cavalry at the front of the English army rushed forward, but they were soon pushed back by the schiltrom hedgehogs.

As these English horsemen fell back, they pushed up against the rest of the English army behind them. They, in turn, were pressed up against the deep marshy waters behind them.

Most of the English archers, or longbow men, were left too far behind to get a good shot at the Scots. When they did fire, they ended up hitting many of their own side in the back.

Edward II's colossal catapults hurled their deadly loads, Greek fire flashed and banged, and killer knights charged to and fro. None of it was enough, though, to make the Scottish hedgehogs curl up in fear.

The Scots believed that the spirits of Columba and other Scottish saints were now right behind them, floating invisibly across the battlefield. This gave the Scots great courage and strength of heart.

Soon the battle began turning against the English.

At just the right moment, Bruce charged into the action with a division of Highlanders and Islanders – which forced the English back even further. Then the king of Scots called on all the common folk he had kept at the rear to join in the attack.

The English saw this and began to panic. Soon the great English army started to crumble – and at that moment its sheer size also became its doom.

As terrified English soldiers ran back from the front, they were like a giant plough that pushed the men behind them into the bog – and down the slopes of a watery stream. A great many English souls drowned in that stream, which was called the Bannock Burn.

Some people might find it strange that the Scots call something that's filled with water a 'burn'. Well, there was no fire in the Bannock Burn – but it was just as deadly. It gave this bloody battle a name that would never, ever be forgotten.

Seeing that all was lost, Edward II fled from the field – taking his royal flag, or standard, with him. This was the signal that England had been defeated.

Protected by 500 knights, Edward II made for safety while the Scots were still busy finishing off his army.

Thousands of English foot-soldiers died, yet many knights managed to ride to safety. Thousands more were taken prisoner by the Scots.

Meanwhile, Edward II reached Stirling and sought refuge in the castle. Incredibly, de Mowbray, the English castle constable, refused to let him in.

De Mowbray knew the Scots would soon be swarming all over the castle, so he decided he would stand a better chance of survival if he told his own king to get lost.

Edward II was forced to race for the safety of Dunbar,

near Edinburgh. There he escaped on a boat south to Berwick.

Bruce had scored a whopping victory over Edward II, and 'sent him homeward to think again', as the song goes. Scotland was free from English slavery (for the moment, at least).

Winning filled Bruce's heart with joy for more personal reasons too. In exchange for English prisoners, Bruce was at last able to free his queen, Elizabeth, daughter Marjorie and sister Mary, as well as the countess of Buchan.

But the war was far from over. Bruce was still cursed by the pope, and his country was in ruins.

Worst of all, though, Edward II would soon want revenge . . .

17

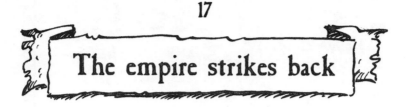

The empire strikes back

Bruce's celebration after Bannockburn didn't last long. He knew that Edward II would soon be back with a new army to try to crush Scotland once and for all.

So Bruce needed to make sure Edward II was kept too busy to invade Scotland again.

A good place to keep Edward II busy was the island of Ireland, which was next-door to England and Scotland. Ireland was ruled by the English, but the Irish people were not happy about this.

This gave Bruce an idea. He sent his last surviving brother, Edward Bruce, across to Ireland in 1315 with orders to start a rebellion against the English.

Bruce reckoned that if his brother could keep Edward II's army busy fighting the Irish, then the English king would have no time to attack Scotland.

At first, things went well. Bruce's brother started a rebellion against Ireland's English rulers, and even declared himself king of Ireland. As planned, the Irish diversion kept Edward II occupied for a while.

But then things started going pear-shaped:

1. The Irish were too busy fighting among themselves to fight the English properly. They made their point by sticking swords in each other.

2. The English rulers of Ireland wanted Bruce's brother to bog off and never come back. They made their point, too – by sticking a sword in him.

Robert the Bruce had even tried going over to Ireland himself to try to sort things out, but it was no use. With Edward Bruce dead, our hero had run out of brothers.

There was no way to keep the Irish diversion going and Bruce was back to square one.

But Bruce's luck was about to get even worse. In 1318 a terrible famine ravaged the land. The Scots began to get stroppy.

Edward II could see the Scots were starving and weary after years of war. He realised this would be a perfect time to strike back, and prepared for a new invasion of Scotland by seizing Berwick.

The English king then sent a letter to Bruce that went something like this:

Dear Robert the Bruce,
You thought you'd sent me homeward to think again after Bannockburn, eh? You thought your little game in Ireland would keep me too busy to invade Scotland did you?
Well, it's time you thought again. I'm going to send a HUGE army to sort you out once and for all.
Unless... you accept that I am the REAL ruler of Scotland. Then I'll spare your life.
love + kisses
King Edward II

Bruce's response to Edward II was simple – 'Get lost!' He rallied his soldiers into action and snatched Berwick back.

So Edward II tried a different approach. He wrote to the new pope, John XXII.

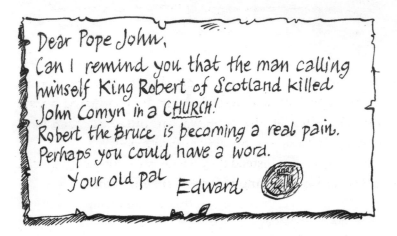

Dear Pope John,
Can I remind you that the man calling himself King Robert of Scotland killed John Comyn in a CHURCH!
Robert the Bruce is becoming a real pain.
Perhaps you could have a word.
Your old pal Edward

Pope John decided that it would be easier all round if Bruce and the Scots just agreed to be conquered by the English. For good measure, the pope declared that Bruce would stay cursed for killing John Comyn until he surrendered.

It looked as though all Bruce's success had been for nothing, and that Scotland was now worse off than before. But the Scots were in no mood to throw away everything they had been fighting for. Instead, they decided to hang up their swords for a bit and try something different . . .

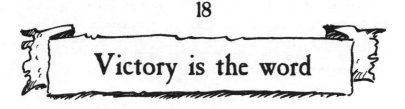

18

Victory is the word

You might think that the Scots should have listened to angry Pope John and agreed to just be conquered by the English. After all, the pope was an influential chap with very special powers. So did the Scots obey?

Of course not. Instead they wrote Pope John very special letters in Latin, asking him to change his mind.

Only one of these letters still survives. It was sent by the Scottish nobles and is called the Declaration of Arbroath.

A declaration means a letter or speech that says something very important. The Declaration of Arbroath is probably the most important letter ever written in Scotland, so it's worth getting to know it properly:

A BEGINNER'S GUIDE TO THE DECLARATION OF ARBROATH

- What is the Declaration of Arbroath? It's a big, dusty Latin scroll with lots of dangly bits at the bottom. The dangly bits are where the Scottish nobles attached their signatures to it, which showed that they agreed with what it said.
- Why is it covered in faded brown tea stains? It isn't. It just looks like that because it's very, very old.
- What does it say? Well, it basically says, 'Dear Pope John, please be nice to Robert the Bruce because he's our king, and we think he's a good guy who deserves to go to Heaven, not Hell.' So it's a plea to Pope John to end Bruce's excommunication, or curse.
- It proves that all the nobles in Scotland really liked Bruce, then? Well, actually no. In fact, some of the nobles who signed it were jealous of Bruce – and later plotted to kill him! Luckily, Bruce found out and locked them up.
- What else does it say? It says the Scots wanted to be 'independent'. Difficult word, simple idea. It means, 'We Scots want to run our own little country by ourselves, so could you please tell the English king and his army to just PUSH OFF and leave us alone?'
- Is that all? No. There's a bit that says, 'There's no way we Scots would let our king, Robert the Bruce, hand Scotland over to Edward II, even if Bruce wanted to.' This meant the Scots would get rid of Bruce if he didn't do what they wanted – a bit like voters would get rid of an unpopular prime minister today. So even in Bruce's day, the Scots had a few ideas about democracy.
- Did anybody else read it besides the pope? Yes, the people who wrote America's famous Declaration of Independence thought it was so great that they borrowed some of its ideas.
- What is it used for now? A mousemat? A drinks coaster? Something to make a paper aeroplane with? Of course not! It's far too precious and important for that, which is why nowadays it's kept safe in the National Archives of Scotland.
- So should we believe everything it says? No, some bits should be taken with a pinch of salt. For example, it includes a bit that says the very first Scot was a girl called Scota, who was a daughter of the pharaoh of Egypt. That legendary story is almost certainly a load of old rubbish – a myth – but many Scots in Bruce's day believed it was true and thought it would impress the pope.

At first, though, the pope wasn't too impressed with the Declaration of Arbroath and all the other fancy letters the Scots sent him.

But after a few years the pope got the message.

Actually, Bruce is a lot less bother than that pain-in-the-backside Edward of England.

Tell Bruce I agree that Scotland is an independent country. Oh, and as a bonus, I'll lift the excommunication – he's no longer cursed.

So the success of the Declaration of Arbroath and the Scots' other letters to the pope prove that it is often better to fight your battles with words rather than weapons.

As the pope began warming to Bruce, Edward II found life much more difficult and his luck began to change for the worse. First, Bruce almost captured him, which forced Edward to make peace with the Scots for thirteen years. Then, after years of annoying his own nobles and courtiers by failing to defeat the Scots and generally being rubbish, Edward got a red-hot poker stuck up his bottom!

That was the end of Edward II, which was good news for the Scots. Edward II's young heir, Edward III, recognised Scotland's independence and Bruce's right to be king. At last, the War of Independence was finally over.

By then, which was 1328, our hero Bruce was starting to get old and frail. It was time for him to start taking things easy.

Bruce went to stay in his retirement home at Cardross, near Dumbarton, in the south-west. Although Bruce didn't have long left to live, he still had time to take care of one last bit of very important business.

19

The last Crusade

If you had seen Bruce when he was an old man, you would have noticed that being a warrior king is not good for your health. Bruce now had one eye socket bigger than the other, lots of missing teeth, a sword scar on his head and a broken cheekbone.

Not that Bruce was all that old when he retired in 1328. He was only fifty-four, but his weary bones had been worn out by battles, hunger and illness.

Then, on 7 June 1329, Bruce took his very last breath – and died. His body was taken to Dunfermline Abbey, the final resting place of kings, and laid in a tomb.

BRUCE'S
LAST
RESTING
PLACES

DUNFERMLINE
ABBEY

BRUCE'S
RETIREMENT
HOME NEAR
DUMBARTON

English chroniclers claimed Bruce had died of leprosy, a horrible wasting disease that makes your flesh fall off – ugh! Yet these reports were probably made up to blacken Bruce's name, so the legend that Bruce died of leprosy may not be true.

If Bruce really did have leprosy, he would have been kept away from other people for their safety – but that never happened. Bruce died of an illness, for sure . . . but exactly what that illness was remains a mystery.

Yet even death was not the end of Bruce's story. Before the king of Scots could finally rest in peace, his heart had one last duty to perform – it would be taken on a Crusade.

So what exactly is a Crusade? A Crusade was a quest by a group of Christian warriors to go and fight in faraway foreign lands against people that they believed were God's enemies.

Usually, that meant anybody that the pope decided he didn't like.

Christians reckoned that God would be very pleased with them for going on a Crusade – and would give them a ticket to Heaven in return.

If Bruce wasn't cursed any more, though, why did he need a ticket to Heaven?

Well, it seems the king was worried that God might still be angry with him over the death of Comyn in a church – despite all of Bruce's great successes since then.

Yet what a success Bruce had been! He died knowing that thanks to him the Scots were no longer slaves to the English.

He had given the Scots freedom to start rebuilding their lives after years of war and hunger. He had also left behind an heir, his little son King David II.

A royal son ensured there would be no empty throne after Bruce died, to which the Scots must have gratefully said, 'Thank God we won't have to go through all that again!'

Yet despite all of this, Bruce was still worried that he had never really pleased God by going on a Crusade.

Bruce had always wanted to go on a Crusade when he was alive, but when would he have found the time? When he wasn't getting rid of the English, he was battering his Scottish foes and rebuilding the kingdom.

The next best thing was for the dead Bruce's heart to become luggage on somebody else's holy quest. So just before he died, Bruce instructed his loyal friend Sir James Douglas to take his heart on a Crusade.

Naturally, Douglas agreed – even though he didn't seem to rate the kingdom of Heaven all that highly. In fact, Douglas once said he personally preferred Berwick town centre!

Despite that, Douglas was the obvious choice for the task of taking Bruce's heart into battle against God's enemies. Years of fighting the English had given Douglas, Scotland's Wild West bandit, an extremely fearsome reputation.

The English called him Black Douglas and English mothers scared the living daylights out of naughty children by telling them:

Even grown men were scared of Douglas. After the Scots won at Bannockburn, some English soldiers were so terrified he might be chasing them that they dared not stop even to have a pee.

Now Douglas's job was to put Bruce's heart in a metal casket, sling it around his neck and go and put the fear of God into some enemy warriors.

The enemies that Douglas was ordered to fight were called Moors. The Moors are not to be confused with Scottish moors, and here's how to tell the difference:

1. Scottish moors are wet, boggy fields covered in heather.

2. The Moors were people. They were not found in Scotland at all, but lived in a part of Spain called Granada.

When Douglas got to Spain, he led an army of Scottish and other knights into battle. Determined to fight to the death, Douglas called on his late great friend and king to lead the way. According to legend, he threw the casket with Bruce's heart onto the battlefield and roared:

So it seems Bruce was the original Braveheart! After shouting these words, Douglas is said to have galloped after the casket and towards his Moorish foes. The Scots were outnumbered – but this time they couldn't beat the odds against them.

Douglas paid for Bruce's ticket to Heaven with his own blood, as he was surrounded and killed by enemy warriors. It was called a heroic sacrifice.

Douglas's body was found by his comrades, boiled in a cauldron of vinegar and his bones returned home to Scotland. Luckily, Bruce's casket was found, too.

The king's heart was brought back to Scotland, where it was buried in Melrose Abbey near the border with England. Bruce was back where he belonged, and able to keep a ghostly watch on Scotland's old enemy – forever.

Epilogue

As the years passed in Melrose Abbey, dust gathered over the place where Bruce's heart lay. As the years turned into decades his old friends, the spiders, spun their cobwebs in the abbey's dark corners.

And as the decades became centuries, bits of Bruce's story got lost or muddled up in the dark corners of people's memories where legends grow. As we have found, there are now a lot of legends about Bruce that are questionable, or wobbly – no doubt like some of his statues.

One great Bruce statue that looks very solid, though, is the giant one of him mounted on a horse at Bannockburn.

The man who made the statue got his hands on a replica of Bruce's skull and used that to make a lifelike model of the king's face. So if you go and look at it, it's almost like seeing the real Bruce. Spooky.

What about Bruce's heart, though? Did everyone just forget about it? Well almost, until a team of experts called archaeologists started digging in Melrose Abbey to see what they could find under the floor.

The archaeologists were amazed to discover a lead casket containing a heart. After some investigating, they agreed the heart must have belonged to Bruce. So they carefully buried the casket again in a special modern tomb.

The ruin of Melrose Abbey is a magical place, and well worth a visit. If you put your ear on the ground at the spot where Bruce's heart was buried, and then listen very carefully . . . you might still be able to hear it beating.